The *Power* of Divine Partnership in Marriages

God's Mandate for Marriage

Mission: To Proclaim Transformation and Truth

Publisher: Transformed Publishing
Website: www.transformedpublishing.com
Email: transformedpublishing@gmail.com
Cover Design: Lily Valley Marketing
Grace Glass
www.lilyvalleymarketing.com

Copyright © 2021 by Teacher Oshowo

All rights reserved solely by the author. No part of this book may be reproduced, stored in a retrieval system, or transmitted in any form or by any means without expressed written permission of the author.

Scriptures are taken from the New King James Version ®. Copyright © 1982 by Thomas Nelson. Used by permission. All rights reserved.

As noted, Scriptures are taken from King James Version (KJV) Public Domain.

ISBN: 978-1-953241-17-7

THE POWER OF DIVINE PARTNERSHIP IN MARRIAGES

✝EACHER

Dedication

To all the married couples within the GLOW.

Glorious Life Outreach Worldwide

Table of Contents

Introduction	1
1: Carrying the Cross of Marriage	5
2: Function According to *Your* Design	13
3: The Holy Spirit is Your Marital Helper	19
4: But First Families	25
5: Through the Lens of Love	33
Let Us Pray	45
About the Author	47

Introduction

Whenever we really want to receive God's will for our lives or enter into next levels, we must prepare to be sacrificial. When a person carries out an assignment, or something they ought to do, with interest and great sacrifice, know that it's someone who's going to have great testimonies.

This is what you see when God wants to lift somebody up. He'll place you in a situation where it seems as if you're leaving everything to do His will. That's a sign He really wants to honor you.

Before you demand for your spouse to treat you the way you want to be treated, you must first be faithful to God by treating your spouse the way the Scriptures say to. There's a recipe that never fails for peace in a divinely arranged marriage. It's in the book of Ephesians.

> Wives, submit to your own husbands, as to the Lord. For the husband is head of the wife, as also Christ is head of the church; and He is the Savior of the body. Therefore, just as the church is subject to Christ, so *let* the wives *be* to their own husbands in everything. Husbands, love your wives, just as Christ also loved the church and gave Himself for her,
>
> Ephesians 5:22-25

A marriage that is divinely arranged by God is the highest level of divine partnership. It *was* the first and it's the best.

The first time God ever partnered anyone on the earth, it was through marriage. In Genesis, the Bible says, God made everything ready for Adam. That means Adam came on the scene and found resources. God even gave him a job. Adam had the instructions. God told him exactly how to *do* what needed to be done; *be fruitful and multiply, subdue the earth and have dominion* (*see* Genesis 1:28).

And the Lord God formed man *of* the dust of the ground, and breathed into his nostrils the breath of life; and man became a living being.

And the Lord God said, "*It is* not good that man should be alone; I will make him a helper comparable to him." Out of the ground the Lord God formed every beast of the field and every bird of the air, and brought *them* to Adam to see what he would call them. And whatever Adam called each living creature, that *was* its name. So Adam gave names to all cattle, to the birds of the air, and to every beast of the field. But for Adam there was not found a helper comparable to him.

Genesis 2:7, 18-20

When God looked at Adam, He saw that he didn't have any suitable partner. The animals were brought to Adam to see what he would call them. A comparable partner was not identified, and Adam yielded each animal to its best possible place of productivity. God wanted Adam to *choose* something suitable for himself. This is a divine key.

†EACHER

Some people miss things and some get things right in their marital journey.

Adam forgot about his own need and did something that was eccentric, foundational, and in line with the divine nature of God *in* him. Adam began to look at every animal God brought his way. He analyzed each and determined which one was *best for this place* and *best for that place.*

He denied his own need and uniquely looked into the need of each animal. At the end of the day, none of those animals had the *best* place by Adam's side. God must have looked at Adam's attention to detail and said, "WOW, that's exactly what I would have done with the animals."

As a result, God cast Adam into a deep sleep and gave him something Adam couldn't have chosen for himself. God brought a partner from the *inside* of Adam to help him with the work God entrusted and assigned to him.

Until God gives you a partner for a divine assignment, He has not yet given the marching orders to carry out *that* assignment. The highest level of partnership is marriage to do the work of the Lord.

1

Carrying the Cross of Marriage

> [S]peaking to one another in psalms and hymns and spiritual songs, singing and making melody in your heart to the Lord,
> Ephesian 5:19

Submission to one another in this verse refers to our attitude towards *ourselves*. That means we must relate with every member in the body of Christ with a sense of divine privilege - a sense of opportunity.

It is God who has given us the opportunity to be fellow church members and fellow prayer partners with each person. We are to interact, in submission to one another, in the fear of the Lord.

Take note – this means God is saying, "In everything you do with this certain person, be conscious of the realization that God is watching over every interaction." The person you're really trying to honor *must* be the Lord. You are honoring that person as a way of showing your respect and honor for the Lord.

Submitting *ourselves* to one another is *not* only reserved for marriage. It also includes our dealings with everyone else we encounter.

In regard to the marriage union, Paul says in Ephesians 5:22, "Wives, submit to your own husbands, as to the Lord."

Excuses many women give include, "Oh, my husband doesn't deserve that level of submission." Or, "Maybe *if* and *when* he submits to the Lord, I'll be submissive to him." While some women see it as, "Oh, if he loves me, it's easy for me to submit to him."

Be aware, the devil is a very cunning devil. There's one way to see it here. I encourage you to simply take God's Word as the final authority in your marital obligations.

It is advisable to only accept the proposal to marry a man who loves the Lord and is submissive to the Lord. This will help you submit more smoothly to your husband.

No matter how seemingly "bad" the foundation of a marriage is, if you really want the marriage to succeed and fulfil the purposes of God, just hold your part of the deal as the husband or the wife. Ask the Lord to help you help your spouse to fulfill his or her part of the deal. Make sure your *own* part of the deal doesn't fail and prayerfully help your partner fulfil their part of the deal within the marriage.

You are individually responsible to God for your part of the deal. God will judge both partners in a divinely ordained marriage individually. He will not blame a wife for the husband's inability to love her sacrificially. He won't say to the wife, "If you'd been a good wife my son would have been able to do his job in the marriage." And God won't blame the husband for the wife's inability to submit.

If you say, "Lord, if you're getting me into this marriage, I want to be sure it's You, so I can honor

You and be loyal to You in this marriage," really make sure God's the One leading you. Once the marriage covenant is entered, there is an expectation of obedience to God's instructions for marriage, in order for it to succeed according to His purpose.

If a person enters marriage because of lust, their own desires, or an emotional decision based on appearances, resources, circumstances, or any other worldly driven motivator, there is *still* no excuse to operate the marriage any other way besides God's way. It's best to say, "Lord, I am committed. I will honor You in this relationship. I will honor You in this marriage."

Wives

You owe God your sacrifice in dealing with your spouse. I am hearing God say this to the wives: *Wives, I'm talking to you now, submit to your own husbands. This is your own part of the deal when you're in a marriage. This is what I expect from you. Submit to your own husbands as if you were submitting to Me. That means, how you deal with them is how I would expect you to deal with Me if I were your husband. Don't deal with your husband only as a reflection of how he deals with you, but as an honorable deed towards Me.*

Knowing God's expectations and having His insight, makes it easier for wives to ultimately treat their husbands the way God Himself wants to be treated.

When I see ladies get involved with men who are not operating by the Spirit and have not matured to the point that they are yielded to the Lord, I just look at the person and think to myself: *This person is entering a difficult life.* God will not say because the man is not a good husband, deal with the man to a lesser degree than the given Scriptural principles for the marriage relationship.

Despite difficulty in marriage, God still expects you to receive strength from Him to carry out His Word in your spouse's life. It's easier for you to submit to your husband as onto the Lord with the right husband - meaning with a man who loves the Lord - a man who treats you as the Lord says a man should treat his wife.

Being in what you may view as a *wrong* relationship, is no excuse to alter God's design, although it may be harder for you to carry it out. God doesn't say, "Okay, I release you from submission because your husband is a difficult man." No, He won't do that. Remember what the Lord says to *all* wives in Ephesians 5:22 - submit to your own husbands, as to the Lord. Wives, do your *own* part of the deal and God will do His. God is fulfilling His promise to take care of you. Listen to the direction of the Holy Spirit, *just focus on your part as onto the Lord.* Let's read further, for clarification:

> For the husband is head of the wife, as also Christ is head of the church; and He is the Savior of the body.
>
> Ephesians 5:23

When God allows you to enter marriage; be sure to reflect your honor for Christ.

It amuses me when a woman goes to church to pray, without making her husband happy at home. Some wives even say to their husbands, "You can't stop me from going to heaven. Whether you like it or not, I'm going to church. You can't stop me from going to church." That's a recipe for trouble. It can cause the very prayers she's going to pray to become vanity and a clanging cymbal.

When a wife takes the time to submit to her husband, and within the window she has, spends time praying also, God is honored. She has given her husband the right level of submission. Within a short time, she is sure to receive the answer to her prayers.

Growing up under a father who is a pastor and being ordained a pastor myself in 2007, I've noticed many married women who pray a lot and attend vigils often, but without their husbands. They look very well put together. When I visit their homes and observe them arguing with their husbands, I no longer wonder *why* their husbands do not come to church gatherings with them. God's instructions have not been obeyed:

> Wives, submit to your own husbands, as to the Lord. For the husband is head of the wife, as also Christ is head of the church; and He is the Savior of the body.
>
> Ephesians 5:22-23

God's desire is for each spouse to show honor for the *Lord* by honoring one another within the divine partnership of marriage. I tell married people and people that are in relationships, "Once you enter a relationship, God wants to see how you honor *Him* through how you treat the spouse He gave to you."

If you chose your spouse for yourself without consulting God or refused His guidance, that doesn't exempt you from the deal or reduce your level of accountability. From now on, treat your spouse how God desires, in order to display your honor towards Him.

2

Function According to Your Design

> Therefore, just as the church is subject to Christ, so *let* the wives *be* to their own husbands in everything.
>
> Ephesians 5:24

I say this respectfully, with honor for all cultures and the laws of every country. A great majority of people *love* their marital partner. But, for the system of God to prevail in your family and to establish a generational commitment to God, your role in the divine marital partnership must be an example to your children.

When you are gone, what kind of family stays? You can enjoy a romantic union with your spouse for 5 years, 20 years, or 30 years and have it just the way you want it. He does all your bidding; she does all your bidding. It's everything you wanted and just the way you wanted it. If you don't follow God's system, all the results that *should* happen in a marriage, the flow of the blessing to your children, may never manifest.

The power of divine partnership in marriages produces well-trained children and a posterity of happiness, joy, and purposeful living from one generation to the next and so on. This generational blessing is built on the foundation of God's principles for marriage.

You will never see a marriage that is *not* built on a sacrificial husband and a submissive wife ever be able to produce children, who *all* walk in the purpose of God and enter godly marriages themselves. When you see a family who has produced a transgenerational level of success extending into the lives of their children's children, that is evidence the husband loved his wife and gave his life for his wife.

Husbands

Some perceive the wife's submission to be more difficult than the husband's role. In this section, we will examine the man's side. God tells husbands:

> Husbands, love your wives, just as Christ also loved the church and gave Himself for her[.]
>
> Ephesians 5:25

While we may see a lot of men telling women, "Submit, submit, submit," that is not the approach God desires. He asked husbands to focus on loving their wives as Christ loved the church and gave Himself for her. That means, Jesus was *willing* to die. Jesus *sacrificially* offered Himself so the church could be born.

This *loving* part is not the part God has given to women. Of course, God isn't saying wives shouldn't love their husbands. The Lord *is* saying He is not looking to see the love of the woman, but rather the love of the man. The love of the man is what God is looking for to bring His backing into the marriage.

For example, if there's only one plate of food in the house and the wife hasn't eaten, the husband shouldn't say, "Oh, I'm the man, I'll eat first." Rather, it is good for the woman to say, "Until my husband comes, we won't eat." It is bad for a man to have a "me first" attitude toward his family. A husband's first concern should be his family. An ideal response may sound like this, "Now that I have come home, is there food for everybody? Alright, why don't you eat first and don't worry, I'll eat later." This is the attitude of sacrificial love. It's not convenient love, it's *sacrificial love*. The kind of love Jesus Christ had for His disciples.

To know how to behave towards women, think about how Christ interacted with His disciples and the instructions He gave:

"By this all will know that you are My disciples, if you have love for one another."
John 13:35

"Greater love has no one than this, than to lay down one's life for his friends.["]
John 15:13

"No longer do I call you servants, for a servant does not know what his master is doing; but I have called you friends, for all things that I heard from My Father I have made known to you.["]

John 15:15

Jesus Christ prided Himself in how He treated His disciples. That's the same level of responsibility and leadership God requests of each husband - *to love and to lead*. For everything that happens to the wife, God wants the man to accept responsibility.

If your wife is sick, you can't go to God and say, "Lord, she has been eating wrong. She doesn't prepare the right meals." Remember in Ephesians 5:23 Paul teaches us the husband is appointed as head of the wife, in the same matter as Christ is the head of the church and the Savior of the body. Your wife shouldn't be sick. Your wife shouldn't have a need.

But if anyone does not provide for his own, and especially for those of his household, he has denied the faith and is worse than an unbeliever.

1 Timothy 5:8

The King James Version of this impartation from Paul to Timothy, and us alike, describes a man who does not provide for his own family as *worse than an infidel*. God respects a man who is doing his best to live for his family.

3

The Holy Spirit is Your Marital Helper

We often hear men say potential wives must bring something to the table. It is okay for a wife to compliment the marriage with her contributions, but really that shouldn't be used as an excuse to neglect God's expectations for the man in marriage.

A man should not use human reasoning to negate the role God has assigned to him with statements, such as, "Oh, she stopped working, now I'm having a hard time paying the bills. If she kept working, I would have been able to take care of the family." If she was working and bringing money home, she did you a favor. She must be appreciated for that favor as long as she lives.

As Christ is the Savior of the body, the man is also the savior of the wife. Husbands who take responsibility for their households come to God and say, "God it was because of me, let judgement pass over my wife. Take my life instead of hers." It's a sacrificial love, quite indescribable to be frank. That kind of man has earned the submission of a woman.

Bible believing women understand how to get the backing of God in their marriage. They know by revelation that a husband doesn't have to *earn* submission. Submission is given as due honor to God. When entering marriage be conscious that the Lord is watching to see how you will honor Him in the marriage. Biblical marriages do *not* go by these concepts: 'if he treats me well, I treat him well,' nor, 'do me as I do you.'

The power of divine partnership in marriages is a *from this day forward* approach, I will be judged by heaven for how I treat my spouse. Therefore, our prayer must be, "Whether it's 20, 30, or 40 years, just give me revelation on how I should treat You, if You were the One I was married to. As You give me the wisdom and grace, I will treat my spouse that way."

Any time there's a difficulty or an argument in the house, wives remind yourselves that submitting to your husband is your devotion towards the Lord.

Don't go around saying to your husband, "The reason I'm not arguing with you is because God said I should submit to you."

No, no, no. Would you tell Christ that? No, receive help from the Holy Spirit to treat your husband as onto the Lord.

Then you may tell the Lord, "Lord, I've done my bid. Help him become a better man. Not just for me, *though it would make it easier for me*, but help *him* so we can be in unity to do more, and we can raise our children right.

A husband or wife, who attempts to negotiate their part of the deal towards God, risks the glorious destinies of their children.

Here are some examples I often share with couples:

Example 1:

Let's say there's a family of six – a husband, wife, and their four children. It's dinner time. There are five pieces of fish available. The husband took three, the wife took a half, and all the children shared the remaining pieces of fish.

The husband took more than 60% of the fish. The rest of the family, which is 80% of the family, then had to divide the remaining 40% of the fish. Obviously, the husband did not practice sacrificial love. This type of selfish behavior hinders the blessing of God from flowing within the family.

Example 2:

A man has four children and one wife. His wife served him dinner. Before enjoying his meal, he asked to see the plates of his wife and children. If he recognized his family had small portions of food and took his own to divide among them so they may have fuller meals; this family, I can expect will have the blessing of the Lord.

My debt to American society is to teach certain principles of God's Word concerning marriage. You must know how practical and easy it is to abide by these principles with the help of the Holy Spirit.

Once accepted, any nation who practices these guaranteed principles will experience supernatural revival. The positive changes that take place in marriages aligned with God's design, not only produce transgenerational benefits to families, but nations. *Yes, you have power in your home to direct the trajectory of nations.*

When God's martial principles are taught correctly, you'll see strong martial foundations built and reestablished. We must help people understand how possible it is, how practical it is, and how beneficial it is to follow Scriptural patterns in their marriages.

4

But First Families

> For the husband is head of the wife, as also Christ is head of the church; and He is the Savior of the body.
>
> Ephesians 5:23

When families do not operate in their roles properly, undesirable issues take root in families, communities, and the body of Christ. Once each person in a family understands their role and that God is omnipresent to help them preform His expectations within the family unit, every other problem will be solved.

A man who focuses on giving to his children first, receives immediate answers of supernatural supply when he prays. This type of demonstration shows the woman that sacrificial love flows from her husband, and she is grateful for him. Before she looks up to heaven to thank the Lord, God has already begun to promote the man.

In contrast, if a man delights in lording over his wife, always demanding her respect and submission, while constantly manipulating the Scriptures to corroborate his point, I can tell his journey will be long. The longer he continues to complain about his wife's lack of submission, the further he heads in the wrong direction.

It would be beneficial for his wife to receive pastoral counseling to encourage her to submit. Whenever a woman comes to me with an issue of this sort, I sincerely find a way to tell her to hold on to her role of submission in the marriage using biblical examples. God always gives more grace to obey His instructions.

I encourage wives that there will always be an open door, an area being neglected, where more can still be done, with the help of the Holy Ghost, even if you married a Nebuchadnezzar (the wicked king of Babylon who took the children of Israel captive).

God allowed Esther to be put into the house of King Ahasuerus, one of the most wicked kings in history, and she still produced Cyrus in *that* house. She was still able to achieve the will of God under *that* man's roof.

If you've entered a marriage, with or without God's consent, you must obey God's instructions:

> Wives, submit to your own husbands, as to the Lord. For the husband is head of the wife, as also Christ is head of the church; and He is the Savior of the body. Therefore, just as the church is subject to Christ, so *let* the wives *be* to their own husbands in everything.
>
> Husbands, love your wives, just as Christ also loved the church and gave Himself for her, that He might sanctify and cleanse her with the washing of water by the word,
> Ephesians 5:22-26

Men, we are leaders. We are representing the Lord, but it's Christ who is the Creator of mankind. He's the Creator of the church. The relationship of Christ and the church, in practice, is not lordship.

We treat Him as Lord, but He doesn't rule over us with tyranny, the way ungodly lords may. He treats us as friends. He treats us as people He's responsible for. He treats us like our lives are His responsibility.

Jesus Christ trained His disciples gently; it's called gentle leadership. *Yes, you can be gentle and still be firm.* Your instructions must be obeyed. The Holy Ghost will help you determine *how* to get others to obey your instructions.

To produce longevity and the power of divine partnership in marriages, an intimacy with God must be developed. Nobody can fully succeed and partake of the full benefits of a divinely ordained marriage without making the Holy Spirit their daily marital helper. The Holy Spirit teaches us how to treat our spouses better, while making us better spouses.

Wives, ask the Lord to help you treat your husband better by developing unconditional submission to him.

Husbands, ask the Lord to help you treat your wife better by developing unconditional and sacrificial love for her.

To the men who are single and trusting the Lord to give them a martial partner, ask the Lord to build in you your own grace, for loving and sacrificing for people, especially for the women around you. Also, pray for the woman the Lord is bringing to you. Say Lord, "Wherever my wife is, teach her this principle of submission as a divine privilege. Help her to understand the benefits of submission, so that when we come together, there will be no hassles."

Since we prefer for God to perfect our spouse *before* the marriage covenant is entered, we must pray for our future spouse, even before we have the realization of who our intended spouse is. In doing this, also know, the marriage covenant is a refiner's fire and God is continually working through His principles to bring forth His will. Preparation is beneficial, but we are continually being perfected. Remember the Holy Spirit is your marital helper.

Once you're already in a marriage, there's no room for debate. Trust the Holy Ghost to change seemingly difficult situations. Proverbs 21:1 says, "The king's heart *is* in the hand of the Lord, *Like* the rivers of water; He turns it wherever He wishes." Do your part of the deal. Carry your cross. Even if you went into the marriage solely by your emotions - *carry your cross!* Carry your cross and submit to your husband. Carry your cross and love the seemingly unlovable. Trust in the Holy Ghost, who is the only One who can truly change a person.

The best thing to do when a woman feels she is not getting love from a man, or a man feels he is not getting submission from a woman to the degree they think they should; is to trust the Lord to lead them to a good church where the pastor teaches the right thing. A church that believes in God's Word.

Open the Scriptures at home and encourage your spouse to join you in a Bible study. Either spouse can initiate the Bible study. Before you study, pray and trust the Holy Spirit to bring up those areas where adjustments are needed – they are throughout the Bible. Love flowing from the husband and submission from the wife, guarantee the power of divine partnership in marriages.

I discovered there's an imbalance in martial relationships when women pursue men solely because they are 'deeply in love'. When I ask couples, "Who loves *more* in the relationship?" And the woman says, "I am the one who loves him more," that marriage is heading toward a crisis. The person who should love more in a martial relationship is the man: *Husbands, love your wives, just as Christ also loved the church and gave Himself for her.*

Age, education level, or financial status should not influence the level of respect a woman gives her husband. A woman *must* respect her husband and respect is not contingent upon any circumstantial factors. Respect is not only for women who see themselves as lower than men, nor because she's younger, less educated, or less financially stable than him. No!

If a man is better than you, richer than you, taller than you, more handsome than you, those things may make it easier to submit, but it would be better that your submission to him flows out of the revelation of what God's Word says.

5

Through the Lens of Love

> [S]ubmitting to one another in the fear of God.
>
> Ephesians 5:21

Wives, make an effort to think to yourself: *Every time he's around, I'll treat him as lord. I'll treat him as master. I'll treat him as boss. I will treat my husband as I would treat Christ if He were physically here with me.*

The Holy Ghost will help you in every situation. Let's look at the following practical example: A couple gets into an argument in the morning before the husband goes to work. The wife was right about the situation, but throughout the day does not have peace. *Why is that?* The wife does not have peace because she was not operating under the guidance of the Holy Spirit in her home. Before reacting to any situation, ask yourself, "Holy Spirit what do I do?"

The Holy Spirit will begin to bring His words into remembrance. The solution in this example, is for the wife to apologize to her husband for delivering her points in such a shattering way, when he returns home from work. She should also explain how she'll find better and healthier ways to get her points across. Responding to conflict in this way allows the Holy Ghost to come in, and over a period of time, He'll make the home pleasant for the two of you to live in harmony.

If a husband is incorrigible and will not bend, overtime, God may take the man away. But as far as God is concerned, the children will be provided for, and the wife will not die in that marriage.

Wives - as much as possible, honor the Lord in submitting to your husband. Husbands - as much as possible, honor the Lord by loving your wife sacrificially.

[T]hat He might present her to Himself a glorious church, not having spot or wrinkle or any such thing, but that she should be holy and without blemish.

Ephesians 5:27

God will judge the success of a married man and the success of his family. What a wife says about her husband is more important than what the church, presidents, governors, or mayors have to say about him.

So husbands ought to love their own wives as their own bodies; he who loves his wife loves himself.

"For this reason a man shall leave his father and mother and be joined to his wife, and the two shall become one flesh." This is a great mystery, but I speak concerning Christ and the church. Nevertheless let each one of you in particular so love his own wife as himself, and let the wife *see* that she respects *her* husband.

Ephesians 5:28; 31-33

These verses are speaking to men. "Let each one of you," that's all men, with individual accountability to God. *A husband who loves his wife, loves himself.* Allow me to say this, the most productive truths of the Scriptures, define the church the most. Defying these truths breeds war, both externally and internally.

The Holy Ghost helps us to accept these truths. It is only the Holy Ghost who can open our eyes to see the benefits of following Christ. Obedience to these principles simultaneously activates the grace that has already been given. Deliverance is produced and with ease the power of divine partnership in marriages becomes more and more evident.

The things that really make Christianity enjoyable are the very same things that bring arguments in Christianity: speaking in tongues, casting out demons, submitting to your husband, loving your wife sacrificially, etc. Being proactive in applying these principles lays a solid foundation for the home. Now the benefits of following God have a place to be showcased.

The blessing of the Lord is guaranteed to overtake those who purposely behave a lifestyle of obedience (*see* Deuteronomy 28:2). It's *not* just praying, fasting, and giving. God has given us practical day to day instructions that must be obeyed. Don't defraud anyone. Give enough labor to your bosses at work. Don't cheat your workers, give them what is due. Answers to prayer show up when Biblical instructions are consistently followed with the help of the Holy Ghost.

God has not, does not, and will not bend His standards. However, He has released help to humanity through the Holy Ghost, who gives us the insight, ability, and wisdom to obey His standards. The relationship between Christ and the church, should be patterned in every situation where a Christian holds a place of lordship.

The behavior of political leaders should replicate the relationship between Christ and the church. As Christ treats the church, according to divine order, is the same way Christians in positions of authority and leadership must treat others. Constituents should be governed in the same matter as a wife. Distinct sacrificial care results in the betterment of that city, state, or nation.

For example, if God knows an armed robber is coming to a house where the man will take a bullet for his wife, He won't allow the armed robber to come. God will never allow a leader over His army, who treats His people the way Christ treats the church, to suffer shame.

Jesus loves and died for *all* people. He told His disciples they would all run away and betray Him that very night. Yet, He prepared Himself to atone the *very* people He knew would eventually betray Him.

> He said to them, "Moses, because of the hardness of your hearts, permitted you to divorce your wives, but from the beginning it was not so. And I say to you, whoever divorces his wife, except for sexual immorality, and marries another, commits adultery; and whoever marries her who is divorced commits adultery."
>
> Matthew 19:8-9

To be quite honest, in the mind of Christ, infidelity isn't a reason for a man to leave his wife. Jesus said it very clearly, to paraphrase, "Moses allowed you to divorce because of your stubborn heart." Then He goes on to say, "except for infidelity, you shouldn't divorce your wife, but from the beginning it was not so." This means, the decision of Jesus Christ is to *stick with people until the end!*

After Peter betrayed Jesus Christ for the last time, Jesus looked at him and Peter burst into tears. The very first person Jesus Christ came to look for when He arose from the grave was Peter. He told Mary Magdalene and the women at the tomb in Mark 16:7, "But go, tell His disciples—and Peter—that He is going before you into Galilee; there you will see Him, as He said to you."

After the resurrection, Jesus met the disciples for breakfast by the sea. Jesus asked Peter to affirm his love:

> So when they had eaten breakfast, Jesus said to Simon Peter, "Simon, *son* of Jonah, do you love Me more than these?" He said

to Him, "Yes, Lord; You know that I love You." He said to him, "Feed My lambs."

John 21:15

Yes, Jesus demanded Peter to reinvoke his commitment to Him once again, but He didn't desert Peter.

My prayer for every married person reading this book is that you won't marry someone who is ever unfaithful to you. But, should it happen, it's not an excuse before the Lord to abandon your part of the deal.

If God gave you *that* spouse, grace is available to heal past the hurt. Be sure to ask for His grace to manifest in each deep place of brokenness. Ask the Lord, "Do You still want me in this marriage?" God will help you, *really* help you, to reconcile with a spouse who betrayed you. Only the Holy Spirt can bring *the* level of restoration, that will dissolve the pain of the wrong from your remembrance. Believe me, there is a certain glory reserved for those who endure hardships until they see revival in their marriage.

Men, when you think about loving a woman, stop thinking merely about how beautiful she is and the emotional and sexual pleasure a woman gives a man. Start thinking about the kind of love Jesus Christ gave for the church.

Whenever you're thinking about leading people politically, being the head of a business or company, do not be entirely driven by profits. It's God's business, He will produce.

Paul said in 1 Corinthians 3:6, "I planted, Apollos watered, but God gave the increase." God will bring the increase. God will bring the honor. He'll bring the glory that comes after you obey Him.

Focus on your responsibility to God to treat each person, including your employer, family members, even those who may have spitefully used you, as Christ treated the church. That means, give them *undeserved* love. Love them far beyond what they could ever qualify for.

As a pastor, over time, I have observed many occasions when people few in number were gathered, yet a strong message was preached. Pastors pray more when there seems to be a lack of commitment. Prayer manifests and strategically drives the Spirit of Christ.

Give more to those you meet on a political assignment, especially when it seems as if they're not responding back. Trust the Lord to bring the reward. The same principles work for employees. Submit to your employer as long as God keeps you there, whether your boss is treating you right or wrong. Give submission to people in authority, as unto God Himself.

> Let every soul be subject to the governing authorities. For there is no authority except from God, and the authorities that exist are appointed by God. Therefore whoever resists the authority resists the ordinance of God, and those who resist will bring judgment on themselves.
>
> Romans 13:1-2

The principle of submission works everywhere! Yield submission and respect to those in authority over you. Refrain from gossiping and mingling with those who do.

Practicing the principles in this book activate the power of divine partnership in marriages. The benefits of perfecting the attributes of God in the safety and sanctity of marriage extend to every other area of life.

Let Us Pray

Before we pray together, take one minute to pray aloud in the Holy Spirit.

Let us pray:

Father, I have honored Your Word and I have taught what you placed in my heart to teach. I ask You to bring out the wisdom of Your Words in a practical way to everyone in their unique situations.

For everyone who picks up this book throughout the ages, I ask that Your wisdom is applied into their hearts. Wisdom that will cause them to *see* what You *say*. Bring forth proof in every level of their endeavor, in the name of Jesus Christ.

Amen

About the Author

TEACHER was ordained a minister of the Gospel of Jesus Christ in 2007. He serves as Resident Pastor of GLOW Nigeria and GLOW International (Glorious Life Outreach Worldwide).

He coordinates GLOW's international ministry with established ministries in North America, Cameroon, Uganda, Zambia, and Kenya.

For additional information or to schedule speaking engagements, please contact:

GLOW International
Email: onegloriouslifeoutreach@gmail.com
Phone: +1-321-615-6315
P.O. Box 236847
Cocoa, FL 32922

God bless you all!

www.ingramcontent.com/pod-product-compliance
Lightning Source LLC
Chambersburg PA
CBHW022231080526
44577CB00005B/179